I'M A GLOBAL CITIZEN

RULES
for
Everyone

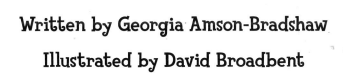

Written by Georgia Amson-Bradshaw

Illustrated by David Broadbent

W
FRANKLIN WATTS
LONDON•SYDNEY

Franklin Watts
First published in Great Britain in 2019 by The Watts Publishing Group
Copyright © The Watts Publishing Group, 2019

 Produced for Franklin Watts by
White-Thomson Publishing Ltd
www.wtpub.co.uk

ISBN (HB): 978 1 4451 6405 2
ISBN (PB): 978 1 4451 6406 9

Series Editor: Georgia Amson-Bradshaw
Series Designer: David Broadbent
All Illustrations by: David Broadbent

Printed in Dubai

Franklin Watts
An imprint of
Hachette Children's Group
Part of The Watts Publishing Group
Carmelite House
50 Victoria Embankment
London EC4Y 0DZ

An Hachette UK Company
www.hachette.co.uk
www.franklinwatts.co.uk

Facts, figures and dates were correct when going to press.

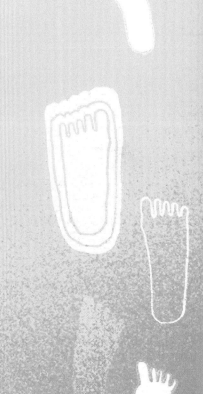

CONTENTS

Look out for this little book symbol to find definitions of important words. Other definitions can be found in the glossary on page 30.

JUSTICE!

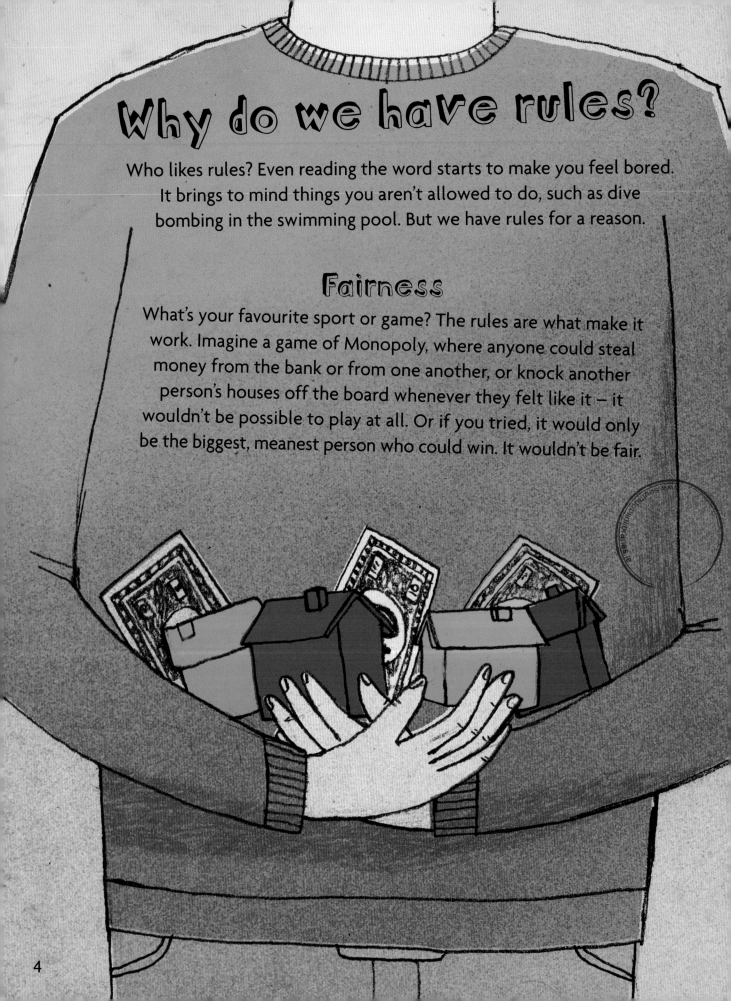

Why do we have rules?

Who likes rules? Even reading the word starts to make you feel bored. It brings to mind things you aren't allowed to do, such as dive bombing in the swimming pool. But we have rules for a reason.

Fairness

What's your favourite sport or game? The rules are what make it work. Imagine a game of Monopoly, where anyone could steal money from the bank or from one another, or knock another person's houses off the board whenever they felt like it – it wouldn't be possible to play at all. Or if you tried, it would only be the biggest, meanest person who could win. It wouldn't be fair.

Safety

As well as keeping things fair, rules keep us safe. An example is the rules of the road – cars have to drive on the correct side of the street, follow the speed limit, and they can't drive on the pavement. If there were no road rules, no one would ever know where a car might come from. And there would be a lot of accidents.

Keeping the peace

Rules help us live together. If there are rules to follow, disagreements are less likely to arise. Think about sharing chores at home. Nobody likes to do chores, but if there are fair and clear rules about who does what and when, there are fewer arguments. When there are no rules, everyone is more likely to argue each time something needs doing – or one person gets stuck doing all the tidying!

Rules we follow

Some rules are written down, and are very specific, with clear punishments for breaking them. Other rules are not written down, and we rely on people following them voluntarily.

School rules

What rules does your school have? Is there a list of them written down somewhere? Normal school rules include things such as being on time for class and not talking during lessons. Which school rules do you think are most important? Are there any you think are not necessary?

Family rules

Our families normally have rules too. These might be less strict than school rules – or maybe not! What rules does your family have? Perhaps you have a bedtime, or a time limit for watching TV. What happens when you break the rules?

Laws

Aside from the rules that we have to follow at school or at home, there are rules that everyone has to follow in society, called laws. The government makes laws for a country. They cover all sorts of things that people must or must not do, from saying people must not steal or hurt other people, to saying they must pay taxes. If someone breaks the law, they might have to pay money or go to prison.

Taxes

Money that people must pay to the government, which the government uses for things such as funding hospitals or schools.

Unwritten rules

As well as clear rules with clear punishments, such as those we follow at school, society has a lot of 'unwritten' rules. These are the sorts of things that make up good manners. For example, it's not against the law to push in to a queue, but it's very bad manners, and the punishment is people being angry with you!

Who makes the rules?

Our behaviour is controlled by the rules that we follow, so it's a good question to ask: who makes the rules, and how? Rules are made by people who have power.

Authority

People who get to make decisions are people in authority. In a school, this might be the head teacher or the school board. At home, parents have authority over children. In society, it's a bit more complicated, but of course the government has the power to do things such as make new laws.

Types of government

A government makes the rules for a country. Throughout history, there have been different types of government around the world. In the past, a lot more countries were governed by monarchies. This means they were ruled by a king or queen, and when that king or queen died, their child usually became the new leader.

Dictatorship

When a country is ruled by one leader who has absolute power, decides all the laws, and doesn't hold elections, it is called a dictatorship. Adolf Hitler (below), the ruler of Nazi Germany (1933–1945), was a dictator. Mao Tse-Tung, who ruled China from 1949 until he died in 1976, was also a dictator. Dictators often use violence and fear to control people, and take away their human rights.

Democracy

Nowadays, many countries in the world are democracies. The idea of democracy is that everyone has a say in what laws we have, through voting. Every adult in the country votes for who they want to be in the government, based on what they promise they will do when they are in charge. The people who win the most votes form the government, and they start making the rules that people voted for. Read more about this on the next page.

How governments work

A government exists to manage a country, a state or a local area. Each level of government has a different amount of power.

Politicians make decisions

Democratic governments are made up of people who have been voted in at election time. Elected politicians make laws and decide how to run things by discussing and then voting on issues among themselves.

Politicians usually each represent a geographic area, and some might have a particular issue that they are responsible for. For example, they might be responsible for how the national education system works, or how the country should interact with other countries.

Election

When adults from a country or area come together and vote on who they want to represent them in government, it is called an election.

Parts of government

Politicians make the laws, but judges interpret the rules that politicians make, and ensure that they are followed. Judges make up the judiciary. Governments also have different levels, from local up to national.

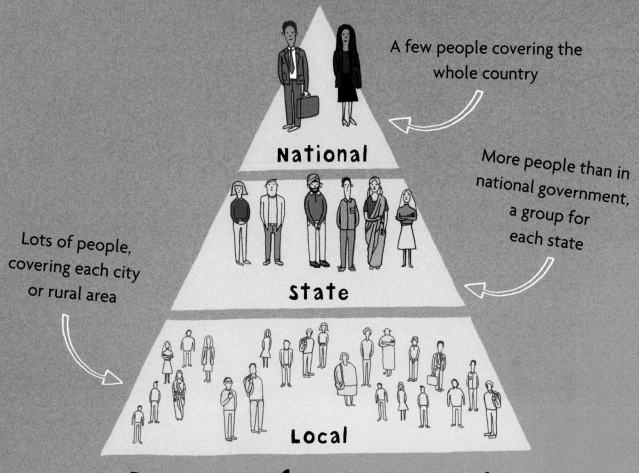

A few people covering the whole country

More people than in national government, a group for each state

Lots of people, covering each city or rural area

National

State

Local

Powers of government

Local governments are only able to make decisions that affect that local area, and most rules and laws are decided higher up. In countries with state governments, decisions about things such as how much tax people have to pay, and how schools are run might be decided at that level. In other countries, those sorts of decisions are made at national level instead, and this varies from country to country.

Knowledge and power

In a democracy, the idea is that the citizens of a country have power through voting. But for that to work, everyone must have a good understanding of the issues that they are voting on. In reality, there are lots of things that can get in the way of this.

Knowledge

It can be difficult to know what the best thing to do is when a problem is big and complicated. It's even more difficult when you don't have all the information. In day-to-day life, most people get their understanding of what is going on in the country through what they see around them, and through the media (such as newspapers, the Internet and TV).

But what if the media doesn't give you all the information, or it gives you misleading information?

One-sided story

Just like people, media companies have a particular point of view. This might mean they prefer one political party or politician over others. So they will often focus more on stories that make the other parties look bad, and their preferred party look good. This is called being 'partisan'.

Even media companies that try not to be partisan cover dramatic stories, such as terrorist attacks, more than less dramatic things such as people dying from disease. This can make it seem like the dramatic events are more common than they really are.

Because of the way the media (deliberately or not) focuses on some stories and not on others, it can make it hard for people to have a good understanding of the issues when they go to vote at election time.

13

Money and power

We've seen how knowledge is important when it comes to who gets to make the rules. But have you heard the saying 'money talks'? Money and power are also closely linked.

Corruption

In the most obvious example, money is linked to power through corruption. A corrupt politician might, for example, secretly take money from someone in exchange for pushing through laws that benefit that person. In countries where there is a lot of corruption, rich people can simply pay politicians to do what they want, against the wishes of the people who voted for them.

Secretly paying politicians is against the law, and in most countries it is not the main way that having money allows people and big businesses to have influence over a country's laws. Instead, it is through perfectly lawful activities that rich individuals and businesses get their way.

Getting elected

In order to get elected, politicians need to get their message out. This means paying for adverts on the TV, and printing lots of leaflets. In some countries, there are limits on how much each candidate is allowed to spend on this sort of thing. In other countries, there is no limit, and more voters are likely to hear the highest-spending candidate's message.

VOTE EMILIO

VOTE EMILIO

VOTE EMILIO

VOTE EM

Donations

Even though bribing (secretly paying) politicians is against the law, it is not against the law to give donations to candidates and parties. But rich people and big businesses aren't going to donate money to candidates promising to do things that they don't like, such as making them pay more tax. Candidates know they are more likely to keep getting the money they need to win elections if they promise to do the things their big, rich donors want.

Unfair rules

What do you think happens when some people have more power to make and change the rules than others? Do you think it leads to situations being fair or unfair?

Changing the rules

Imagine you had the power to make all the rules at school. What would you do? You could make everything very fair, for example saying that everyone had the same amount of break time and had to wear the same uniform.

Or you could make things less fair. You could make a rule that said you and your friends were allowed longer breaks than everyone else, or that other students had to do your homework for you.

In reality, some people do have more power to influence the rules than others. By shutting some people out of making decisions, it leads to unfair situations.

Colonisation

One example of unfair situations created when power is unevenly shared is colonisation. This is when one country invades and takes over another country, such as when Britain took over India in the nineteenth century. When Britain ruled over India, they made all the rules, and took money and goods out of the country and back to Britain. The country of Britain became rich, while the Indian population did not have many rights.

For example, the British put a very high tax on people making salt from seawater in India. The British made salt too expensive for many Indian people. But the Indian people had no power to change the rules the British made until they won their independence in 1947.

TAKING BACK POWER

Have you ever heard the phrase 'there's strength in numbers'? In many unfair situations, there are small numbers of rich, powerful people in control, making the rules. But when ordinary people join together, they have great power.

Changing minds

People have different ideas about some rules. For example, people can feel strongly about laws that allow gay people to get married. Campaigning organisations can change people's minds, alert people to important issues and unfair situations, and encourage them to vote for political change. In Australia in 2017, after a nationwide survey, a campaign successfully got the law changed to allow gay marriage. Many of the people involved had never campaigned before.

Civil disobedience

Ordinary people who come together can achieve a lot through simply refusing to follow unfair rules. Remember the Indian people who were not allowed to make salt (page 17)? In 1930, Mohandas 'Mahatma' Gandhi led a march to the sea to make salt without paying the tax.

Gandhi and the Indian people's salt march sparked millions of other acts of civil disobedience around the country. It took 17 years, but eventually the scale of protest within India meant that in 1947 the British had to leave. The Indians were then able to elect their own, democratic government, and decide on their own rules.

Revolution

In some situations, people have had no choice but to take up weapons and fight for their rights. During a revolution in Haiti from 1791 to 1804, black slaves of mostly African origin rose up against their cruel, white French masters.

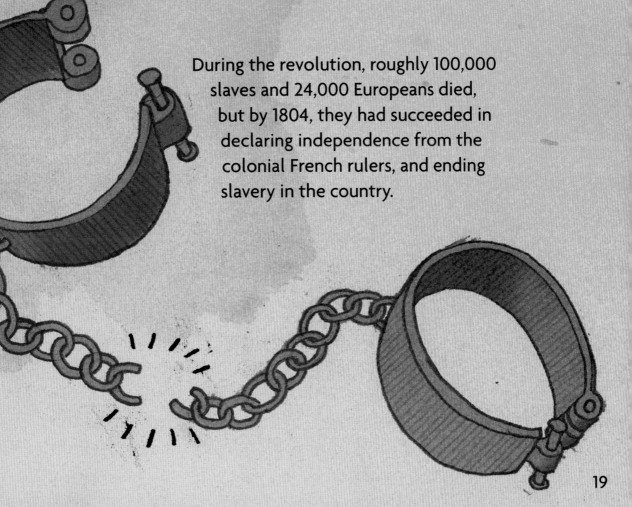

During the revolution, roughly 100,000 slaves and 24,000 Europeans died, but by 1804, they had succeeded in declaring independence from the colonial French rulers, and ending slavery in the country.

A taste of power

How does the amount of power someone has affect their ability to make the rules? Play this game to find out. Grab a group of at least six friends, something to act as a spinner and a couple of packets of sweets.

Round one

Put out the same number of sweets as you have players. Discuss among you how you think the sweets should be shared. Once you all agree how many sweets each person gets, divvy them up.

Round two

Put out a new pile of sweets. This time, put out only half as many sweets as there are players. Two players (selected randomly by the spinner) are 'politicians'. One player is 'the media'. Each of the politicians gets to argue how they think the sweets should be allocated. The media gets to say which politician has made the best argument and why. No one else gets to say anything. After each speech, all of the players vote on which of the two proposed ways of dividing the sweets they agree with. (Note – sweets can't be cut up.) Everyone gets one vote, and the sweets are divided according to the winning proposal.

Round three

Repeat round two, randomly choosing three new players to be the politicians and the media. But this time, the number of sweets a player has equals their number of votes. So if a player has three sweets already, they get three votes. If they have no sweets, they get no votes.

Round four

Put out the same number of sweets as there are players. Spin the spinner to select your politicians and media, and give the sweets directly to both politicans, dividing them up between the two of them. If the sweets don't divide evenly, give the extras to the media. This time, only the media gets to make an argument for how the sweets should be divided, but no one votes. It's up to the two politicians to decide whether or not to share their sweets out or not.

Making change happen: Aboriginal civil rights

Indigenous Aboriginal people had lived in Australia for around 60,000 years before the British arrived in the eighteenth century and took over their lands. As many as 90 per cent of the indigenous population died in the 10 years after British settlement due to violence and disease. Those who survived were not treated as equal citizens, and had no rights.

Aboriginal Protection Act

The British enforced extremely strict and unjust rules on the lives on the indigenous people. In the state of Victoria in 1869, the Aboriginal Protection Act was brought in to control the lives of indigenous people. This law regulated where they could live, what jobs they could do, who they could marry and be friends with and other aspects of their daily lives. Laws like this were put in place all over Australia.

The stolen generations

The law also gave the Australian government the right to take indigenous children away from their parents, and put them in care homes or give them to foster families.

Indigenous activism

During the 1950s and 60s, indigenous people began campaigning against the breaking up of families, and the racist, unfair rules that completely controlled their lives. Activist Faith Bandler co-ordinated a campaign including several massive petitions. In 1965, the group Student Action for Aborigines (SAFA), led by third-year student Charlie Perkins, organised a bus tour that aimed to reveal the terrible conditions indigenous people lived in.

Change begins

In 1967, a vote was held to change the Australian Constitution to remove parts that discriminated against indigenous people. Ninety per cent of the Australian population voted in favour. Although this did not immediately change indigenous peoples' living conditions, it led to further changes to the law. By the early 1970s, the practice of removing children was abolished. In the 1980s, land began to be returned to indigenous ownership.

STUDENT ACTION FOR ABORIGINES

Profile: Dejusticia plaintiffs

Around the world, many governments have sets of rules called constitutions, which lay down the rules that say how the country will be organised, and how it will protect its citizens. But sometimes, the government doesn't follow the rules – so what do you do then? In Colombia, 25 young people tackled that problem.

Eight-year-old Acxan Duque Guerrero lives in Buenaventura, Colombia. He's a scout, and loves playing football. Aymara Cuevas Ramírez, also aged eight, has been a nature lover from a very young age. She's part of a gardening club at her school in Itagüí. Thirteen-year-old Pablo Cavanzo Piñeros lives in Bogotá, the capital of Colombia, but his favourite hobby is to go walking and camping in the Colombian forests.

Acxan, Aymara and Pablo are three of the 25 children and young people who, with the help of the organisation Dejusticia, took the Colombian government to court in 2018, and won. They argued that the Colombian government wasn't following constitutional rules that said every Colombian citizen must have access to a healthy environment, life, food and water.

Despite signing up to international agreements to reduce climate change, the Colombian government had not reduced deforestation in the Colombian rainforest. Deforestation contributes a lot to climate change and reduces the supply of clean water. The young plaintiffs argued that deforestation and climate change are threatening their health and safety, and it would get even worse in the future.

The judges agreed with the young plaintiffs that by allowing so much deforestation, the government had not been obeying the most important rules in the constitution about protecting their rights. The judges gave the government four months to put an action plan in place to stop people cutting down the forests.

Activate!
Make a campaign video

Young people might not be able to help change the rules through voting, but they can still campaign and try to influence other people's choices. Nowadays, a lot of the information we get about news, politics and the world is through social media. Videos are particularly good at catching people's attention online – so why not make a campaign video?

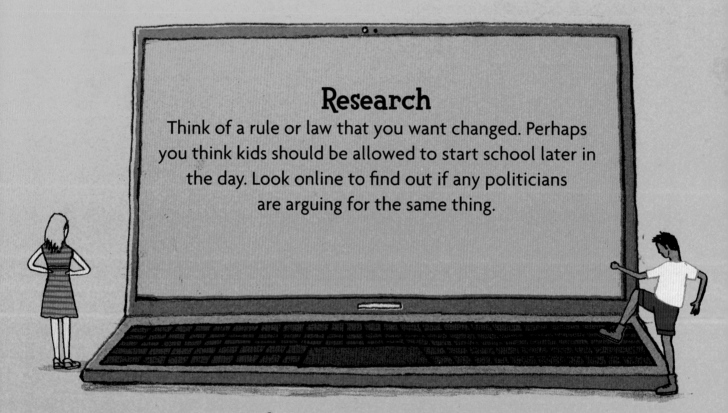

Research
Think of a rule or law that you want changed. Perhaps you think kids should be allowed to start school later in the day. Look online to find out if any politicians are arguing for the same thing.

Get to the point
People don't have very long attention spans when watching things on social media, so plan your video to be no longer than 60 seconds. You want to make your message very clear, so explain as simply as possible which rule you want changed, and why.

Use emotion

It's good to use statistics or facts to back up your argument, but only use one or two hard-hitting ones, or people will switch off in a barrage of numbers. As well as stats, it's important to appeal to people's emotions. If possible, tell a personal story about why changing that rule or law is important to you.

Call to action

Make sure you finish your video by saying what people should do to make a difference on this issue. Perhaps you want them to vote for a particular politician at election time, or maybe tell them to email their local representative on the topic.

The tech

It's easy to record your video on a smartphone, then upload it to social media. If you want, you could take it a step further by using some video editing software to add other images or background music to your video.

But always ask permission from an adult before making and uploading your film.

Organise!
start a debate club

Being able to convince people of your point of view is a very powerful skill if you want to change the rules. But at least as important is being able to understand why other people hold their points of view. A great way to get better at both of these things is debating – so why not start a debate club at your school?

what is a debate?

During a debate, you have two opposing sides. A statement is proposed by 'the house', such as 'This house believes the law should change to allow children to watch 15- and 18-rated films at the cinema'. One side is arguing for the statement (so, agreeing that kids should be able to watch the films), and the other side is arguing against (they should NOT be allowed).

The two sides take it in turns to make their argument, then take questions from an audience who are watching, or from a panel of judges. At the end, either the audience votes for which side was more convincing, or the judges decide.

TEAM A

Skills

Debating is great for making you more confident at speaking in public, helping you build convincing arguments, read people's reactions and listen to other people's points of view. It's also very satisfying to win a debate!

Getting started

To start a debate club, you'll need at least seven people to come regularly. That's two teams of two people, and three to be the audience/judges.

Before getting into debating proper, there are lots of fun games you can play to start developing your skills. Research 'start a debate club' on the Internet to find lots of websites with activity ideas, and instructions on how to hold a formal debate.
Once you've got the hang of it, you could enter your team into a national competition!

TEAM B

Glossary

Aboriginal Australians people living in Australia who are descended from people who have always lived in Australia, before Europeans arrived in the 18th century

activism to campaign for social change

authority a person or organisation who has the power to make the rules and control others' behaviour

candidate someone hoping to be elected

citizen someone who is legally recognised as living in a particular country

civil disobedience refusing to comply with certain laws that are considered unjust, or to protest peacefully about unjust laws

colonisation the process of invading and taking over another country or area

constitution a set of political principles or rules by which a country is governed

corruption dishonest or illegal behaviour by people in power, usually involving being paid money

deforestation the cutting down of forests

democracy a type of government meaning 'rule of the people', where the citizens of a country vote regularly for who they want to be in charge

dictatorship a type of government where one person or a small group of people are in charge, with no restrictions on their power

donation a gift of money, often to a political party or organisation

gay someone who is attracted to people of the same sex

government a government sets and controls the laws within a country, state or area

indigenous people descendants of people who have always lived in a particular area

judiciary the system of law courts in a country where judges review and enforce laws

law a rule that everyone must follow or be punished by the state (such as by going to prison or being fined)

monarchy a type of government where a king or queen rules, and when they die their children usually take over

revolution the overthrow of the government by the people who are ruled, perhaps violently

statistics facts and figures that show data, such as how often things happen, or how likely something is to occur

tax money that people have to pay to the government to fund things paid for by the government, such as schools, hospitals or the army

voting formally choosing who you want to be in charge in an election

Further information

How to Build your Own Country
by Valeria Wyatt (Wayland, 2015)
Learn about the UK government and political systems by designing your own country from scratch.
Decide on laws, figure out how to raise money, and how to interact with neighbouring countries.

Vote for Me! Democracies, dictators and decision-makers
by Louise Spilsbury (Wayland, 2017)
Read about the different systems of leadership that exist around the world and throughout
history. What are the different ideologies or worldviews that different governments have? What
sorts of leaders are there, and how do they get power?

A Peaceful World
by Alice Harman (Franklin Watts, 2019)
Discover more about Gandhi, protest and power in this book about peace and conflict.

Websites

youtube.com/playlist?list=PL03FFE1F0B34AA057
Watch videos about how the UK parliament and democracy work, covering topics such as 'How
does the General Election Work' and 'Introduction to the House of Commons'.

bbc.com/bitesize/topics/zxvv4wx
Watch a video about debating on the BBC bitesize website, then try a quiz to test your knowledge.

parliament.uk/education/teaching-resources-lesson-plans
On the UK government's educational website, find all sorts of resources about how the UK
parliament works, as well as important and inspiring people such as the suffragettes.

Note to parents and teachers: every effort has been made
by the Publishers to ensure websites are suitable for children,
that they are of the highest educational value, and that they
contain no inappropriate or offensive material. However,
because of the nature of the Internet, it is impossible to
guarantee that the contents of these sites will not be
altered. We strongly advise that Internet access is
supervised by a responsible adult.

Index

I'M A GLOBAL CITIZEN

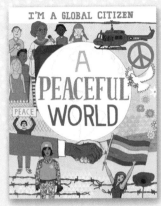

978 1 4451 6401 4

978 1 4451 6399 4

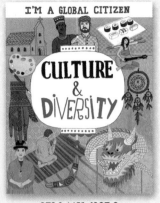

978 1 4451 6397 0

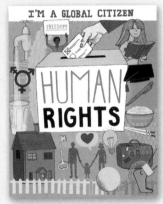

978 1 4451 6403 8

978 1 4451 6405 2

978 1 4451 6362 8

Series contents lists

A Peaceful World
- What is peace?
- What is conflict?
- Why is peace important?
- What causes conflict?
- Keeping the peace
- Working it out
- An unfair fight?
- Consequences
- Negotiating peace
- Making change happen: Indian Independence
- Profile: Leymah Gbowee
- Activate! draw a peace path
- Organise! a day of peace

Caring for the Environment
- What is the environment?
- What is climate change?
- Living in a changing climate
- Losing living things
- Be a bee
- Problems with pollution
- One planet living
- Big green quiz
- What is environmental justice?
- Making change happen: The Paris Agreement
- Profile: Wangari Maathai
- Activate! be a photojournalist
- Organise! eco challenges

Culture and Diversity
- What is culture?
- What is diversity?
- What's YOUR culture?
- Multicultural life
- Prejudice and discrimination
- Discrimination in society
- Where on Earth?
- Seeing things differently
- Wheel of life chances
- Making change happen: Apartheid in South Africa
- Profile: Bolivia's 'Cholitas'
- Activate! act against racism
- Organise! put on a culture day

Human Rights
- What are human rights?
- What is the Universal Declaration of Human Rights?
- Are human rights different for children?
- Why might people's human rights not be respected?
- What happens if human rights aren't respected?
- Connected human rights
- Rights and restrictions
- The limits of human rights
- Making change happen: Black Lives Matter
- Profile: Kailash Satyarthi
- Activate! make a human rights wall
- Organise! a human rights rally
- Universal Declaration of Human Rights

Rules for everyone
- Why do we have rules?
- Rules we follow
- Who makes the rules?
- How governments work
- Knowledge and power
- Money and power
- Unfair rules
- Taking back power
- A taste of power
- Making change happen: Chile's 'No' campaign
- Profile: Aruna Roy
- Activate! make a YouTube campaign video
- Organise! start a debate club

We're All Equal
- What is equality?
- Inequality around the world
- We're all equal ... or are we?
- Why is equality important?
- Does equal always mean fair?
- Sweetie-sharing challenge
- The game of inequality
- Picture this
- Let's roll
- Making change happen: votes for women
- Profile: Malala Yousafzai
- Activate! make equality infographics
- Organise! hold an equality day

FRANKLIN
WATTS

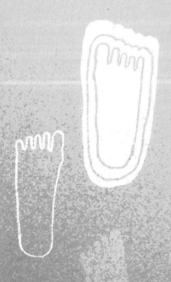